AuthorHouse™
1663 Liberty Drive
Bloomington, IN 47403
www.authorhouse.com
Phone: 1 (833) 262-8899

This book is printed on acid-free paper.

ISBN: 978-1-7283-7013-2 (sc)
ISBN: 978-1-7283-7014-9 (e)
ISBN: 978-1-7283-7012-5 (hc)

Library of Congress Control Number: 2020915126

Print information available on the last page.

Published by AuthorHouse 09/09/2020

authorHOUSE

Even if at rise and shine, you spill your milk at breakfast time...

When you
forget to
feed the
cat

Or miss the ball
when you swing
the bat ...

When you leave your
clothes on the floor
And when you slam
the bedroom door...

If you don't get
an A on a test
or stay up late
without your rest...

If ever you think
the rules are not
fair
Or that the world
does not care ...

Through times of sass
tantrums and chat—
Even when you act
like that ...

I love you for all
that you are and
all that you do...

If you make a mistake or eat the last piece of cake ...

On days the clouds
cover the sun,
You will still be
my Number One!
and ...

Every bit of who you are
and every part of you
I see reminds me that God
made you perfect and
exactly how He wants
you to be and ...

Your smile, your heart
and your loving soul
Will be with you
Wherever you go
And . . .

The world may try to
take your smile and
get you off track for
a little while but I'll be
here to help you get
your smile back.

Never forget whether
near or far
that...

I love you
for every
Wherever you are.

Printed in the United States
By Bookmasters